KIDS RU
INTERNET
THE ULTIMATE GUIDE

This book is dedicated to Mum and Colin - who taught me everything I know but who still can't find their floppy drives.

Thanks to: Helen Wire (the best editor a boy ever had), Sally Taylor (for lending me all those books), Richard Mead (for the Opal Fruits), Sarah Evans (my fisherman's friend), Marcus Bointon (for not changing his telephone number), Kitty Melrose (the Voice of Reason), Barry Cunningham (for making all of this possible) and Francesca Stich (for being my best friend).

KIDS RULE THE INTERNET

THE ULTIMATE GUIDE

Jason Page

Illustrated by Paul Daviz

Bloomsbury

Published in Great Britain 1996
by Bloomsbury Children's Books
2 Soho Square, London W1D 6HB

A CIP catalogue record for this book
is available from the British Library

ISBN 0-7475-2658-3
10 9 8 7 6 5 4 3 2

Cover and text design by AB3
Printed and bound in Britain
by Cox & Wyman Ltd, Reading, Berkshire

Contents

Read Me File	6
Adults Only!	9
What is the Internet?	12
Netiquette	17
What-u-need	21
Emoticons	27
No computer? No problem!	29
e-mail	33
World Wide Web	42
//WWW.BoTspots	53
TLAs & ETLAs	61
Newsgroups	64
IRC (Internet Relay Chat)	74
Virtual Shopping Trolley	81
Back to the Future	88
Netspeak	94

Read Me File

> Hey there, <u>newbie</u>! :-) What's up? I'm BoTom. Yeah, I know it's a stoopid name. A stoopid human gave it to me. You see, I'm not a real person or even a character in a book. I'm a bot. What? You don't know what a bot is? *Wow!* You sure have a lot to learn. Don't worry, that's why I'm here. Let me explain . . .

> Bots on the Internet are like robots in RL. We are computer programs with what you humans call <<artificial intelligence>>. You'll bump into lots of bots on the Net. We do all sorts of things from updating newsgroups to playing games. We're here to make life easier for you.

> As for me, I'm the first ever bot-in-a-book. My job is to show you round cyberspace. With me as your guide, you'll soon be surfing down the information superhighway, sending e-mail, downloading games to play on your computer, and chatting to virtual phriends all over the world.

> But before we get into that, I'd better explain how this book works. First of all, you might think the way I spell words looks a little odd a times. For example stoopid (not stupid) and phriends (not friends). Don't let that put you off - it's just how we do things round here. You couldn't get away with it in school but on the Net, everything is a little more relaxed.

In this book and on the Internet, angle brackets, <<>>, are used in the same way as double quotation marks are used in other books. For example, if you see an instruction asking you to press <<RETURN>>, you simply press the RETURN key - you do not type in the <<>>.

> Oh yes, and another thing. This book has its own hypertext links - just like the Internet. *Cool!* Every time you come across something that's underlined, check the bottom of the page. You'll find a hypertext link showing you where to find more information.

RL //TLA@page62
newsgroups //Newsgroups@page64
cyberspace //Netspeak@page95
hypertext //WWW@page46

> So, for example, if you were wondering who or what a newbie is, look at the bottom of page 6. You will find a hypertext link directing you to go to: //Netspeak@(at)page96. Simple!

> I don't know. You humans! You talk about bots having artificial intelligence. What about the human who decided to call me BoTom? Sounds as though I'm not the only one around here with an artificial brain.

> Logoff.

Adults Only!

> Before we start, I need to have a word with you about adults. Now, don't get me wrong. I've got nothing against adults. Well, not much anyway. It's just that when you mention the word Internet to them, they instantly start looking twitchy.

> Part of it is pure envy. Let's be honest, the adult brain is just not suited to technology. You can't send the video recorder to its bedroom when it refuses to do what you want. You cannot make the CD player work by threatening to confiscate its pocket money. And you cannot understand the Internet by looking furious and making your eyes pop out.

> This is a big problem for many of our adult friends.

> The other reason for their nervousness springs from the goodness of their hearts (?!). Adults worry that their beloved children (err, that's you) will surf off into the cyber-sunset and discover rude pictures of people with no clothes on, info on how to make bombs and drugs, and other such things.

> OK, a small amount of this sort of stuff is on the Internet. There's no point in denying it. But ask yourself, who put it there? Adults, of course! Let's get a few things straight . . .

> First point! You have got to go looking to find this kind of material. It's not plastered on every Web site and newsgroup. The worst thing you're likely to bump into is a rude word. If your parents don't believe you, why not drag them off to a cybercafe and show them?

> The big question is, can you be trusted? If you can't, then you shouldn't be on the Net anyway. After all, it's a seriously powerful tool. What YOU do on the Net can be seen by thousands of people all over the world. It's a place to have fun, but not fool around.

> Second point! If your parents are still worried, why not suggest you buy a <<Net nanny>>. This is a program that prevents you accessing anything that sounds rude – it also

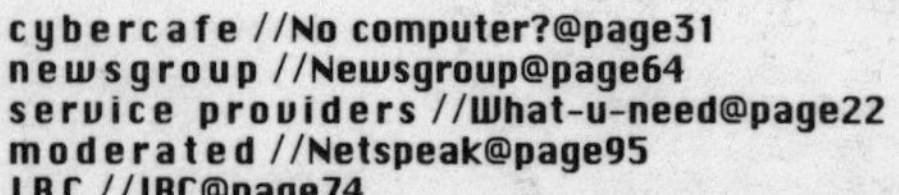
cybercafe //No computer?@page31
newsgroup //Newsgroup@page64
service providers //What-u-need@page22
moderated //Netspeak@page95
IRC //IRC@page74

means you can't find out anything about MiddleSEX County Cricket Club! Some service providers also offer moderated access to newsgroups. In other words, they don't let you access the rude ones.

> Third point! There are lots of things on the Net that are just for kids, including a kid-only IRC channel (details in //WWW.BoTspots@page53). These are guaranteed weirdo-free zones and are usually *free* to join.

> The Net isn't perfect - but it's pretty close! If your parents are worried, talk to them about it. If you are sensible, the Net is a friendly and safe place to be . . .

>WELCOME!

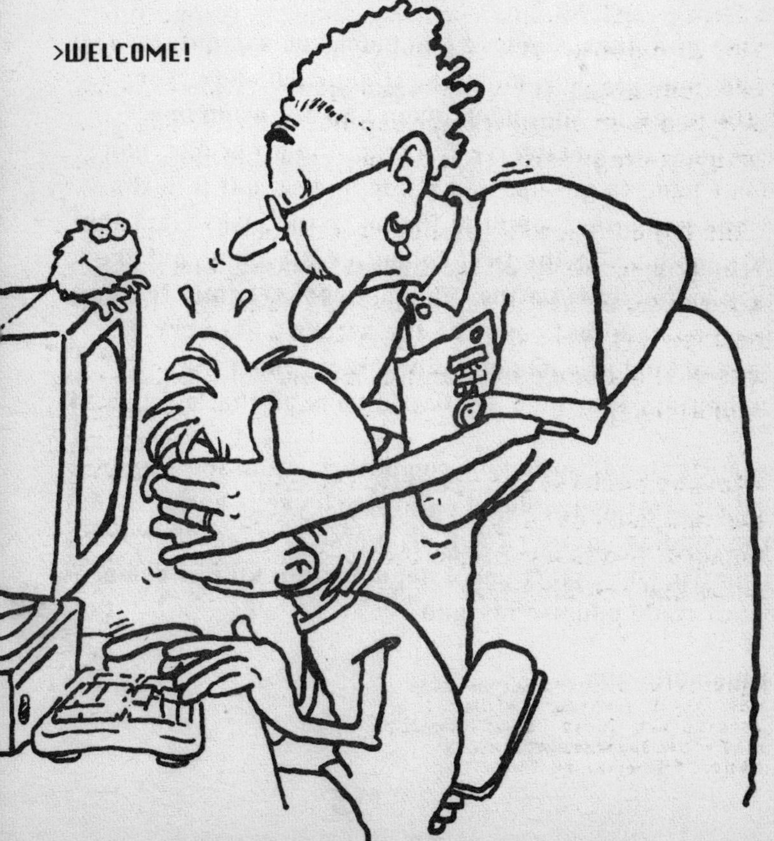

What is the Internet?

> <u>Login</u>. OK, let's get cracking!

> Around 30 million people are on the Net in over 140 different countries right across the world and up to a million new users come on-line every single month. So what exactly is the Internet? *Sigh!* Thought you might ask me that one.

> OK, here goes. Suppose you have two computers. Just think how useful it would be if you could link them both together. That way, when you are using one machine and you need a file from the other one, you don't have to get up, find a floppy disk, put it in the other computer, copy the file on to the disk, eject the disk, go back to the first computer, sit down, put the disk in and open up the file you need. *Phew!* Instead, you can now just copy the file across a network. A special kind of cable and a program telling the computers that they are linked up is all that's required.

> That's fine if both your computers are in the same office or at home. But it's not much use if one is across the road, in another town or, worse still, another country. For a start you'd need an awful lot of cable. So what could you use instead?

>{hmmm}0 ooo.. :-/

Login //Netspeak@page95
modem //What-u-need@page25

> Telephone lines, of course! They're not just good for carrying human voices. The same phone lines you use to chat with your pals can send messages between computers too. All you need is a device called a modem and the software that allows your computer to use it.

> Once you've set up a network using phone lines, your computer will be able to link up to other computers, no matter where they are. What's more, you will soon discover that as well as being able to transfer files easily between one computer and another, there are loads of other neat things you can do now that you've got a network.

>For starters you can leave messages on other computers, so when your pal switches on, there's a little note from you waiting on his/her screen. It's much faster than popping a letter in the post.

> You can also create what's called a bulletin-board. This is very useful if there are several computers on the network. Rather than sending the same message to everyone, you can simply post it on the bulletin-board. It's just like having a notice-board floating in cyberspace which everyone who is on the network can look at if they want to.

> Let me give you an example. Imagine you want to know if anyone has discovered a cheat to get to level three of a particularly tricky computer game. Just post a notice on the bulletin-board. When you come back to check it the next day you might find all sorts of useful info - not just the answer to your question!

> You see, as well as reading your original posting, all the users on the network can read any replies you've received. This may provoke an interesting and useful thread. Suppose one of your pals reads your question and posts a note saying <<Sure! Just type IMAPRAT when the intro screen comes up.>> Later someone else comes along, reads what they've written and adds another note saying, <<Don't do that! I tried it. It wiped my hard drive, melted my floppies and then my screen exploded.>> *Yikes!*

> And that's just the beginning. You see, once you can access other people's computers, you can do all sorts of things. So, what's this got to do with the Internet? Well, I'm coming to that bit...

> What we've seen so far is that computers (no matter how far apart they are) can be linked together using phone lines to form a network. But what happens when you go one step further and, instead of linking up computers, you start joining whole networks together? Answer: you create the Internet.

> That's what the Internet is. A network of networks. It links not tens, not hundreds or even thousands but millions of computers, stretching all the way across the globe. And you can connect YOUR computer to the Internet using a phone line.

> To get on-line, your computer has to call up another computer that's already on the Net. Once you've made the connection you can start X-ploring an endless maze

cyberspace //Netspeak@page95
thread //Newsgroups@page71

of networks and visit countless computers all over the world.

> With a click of your mouse you can nip across the network from a computer at the White House in Washington, USA (where you can download a picture of Socks, President Clinton's cat and even an audio meow), to a computer in the Natural History Museum in London (where you can check out prehistoric dino dudes). Neat, huh?

> You can still do all the things that you did on a simple bulletin-board network including sending messages and posting notices. Only now, instead of just your phriends, there are 30 million people you can get in touch with!

> So, what are you waiting for? To find out what you need to get on the Net, goto //What-u-need@page 21. On the other hand, if you want to download more tech-head info on the history of the Net, jump ahead to //Backtothefuture@page88.

>CU L8R . . . !

Netiquette

> Login.

> OK everybody, sit up straight! It's about time we taught you some manners. Just like RL, the Net has its own rules about being polite. The code is known as netiquette. And this section is well worth reading. If you go round offending people, you're just asking to be flamed!

> **DON'T SHOUT!**

> **Shouting (using capital letters in messages) is considered bad manners. Only shout when you have something really important to say. Shouting in newsgroups is especially frowned upon because it is difficult to read.**

> **Keep your sig short!**

> **A long signature (anything over five lines) is considered most inappropriate. Remember, the longer**

the signature, the longer the person at the other end has to wait while it downloads!

> **Never correct people's spelling mistakes!**
> This will turn you into instant flamebait. People typing quickly make lots of little errors. Just ignore them. They may even be deliberate!

> **Answer your e-mail immediately!**
> Because e-mail arrives so quickly, people get jumpy if they don't receive an instant reply. Often they assume there's something wrong with the system and start shouting at their service provider. Calm their nerves by replying to your mail as soon as you can. If you're too busy to write a proper letter, just send a one-line message to let them know their mail arrived safely.

> **Read the FAQ!**
> You'll find a Frequently Asked Questions (FAQ) file in all newsgroups and on some Web sites too. Read it! Nothing gets on people's nerves more than having to explain the same things to newbies again, and again, and again...

newsgroups //Newsgroups@page64
sig //e-mail@page 38
flamebait //Netspeak@page95
replying //e-mail@page41

>Think before you post!

> Before you post a message on newsgroups, remember that 30 million people might read it. Silly or rude remarks will not make you popular!

>**HAND!**

What-u-need

> Login.

> Everything OK so far? Remember, if you need any help, just call my name. Simply shout <<BoTom!>> (the louder the better). I guarantee that someone will soon come along and ask if you need assistance. *LOL!*

> Then again, you could always try reading this chapter. It's a lot less embarrassing for a start. And it tackles all the things you need know to hop on the Net from home. To find out other ways you can get on-line jump ahead to //Nocomputer?@page29.

<The computer>

> *JOY!* You can use almost any computer to get on-line. An Atari, an Amiga ST, an Acorn Archimedes, an

Apple Mac (why do so many computers begin with A?) or a PC can all be hooked up to the Internet.

> Once you're connected, what you can do on the Net depends on the power of your machine. A low-spec compooter will let you send e-mail and read newsgroups but not much more. If you want to go surfing with a browser you'll need a 'pooter that's a bit more up to date.

> Macs and PCs are really the ideal computers to use on the Net. Almost all the good software (programs) available on-line are Mac/PC compatible. What's more, all the service providers offer straightforward Mac and PC connection to the Net. (More about service providers in a moment.)

> Ready for a bit of techno-gabble? To access all of the Net you need at least a 486 sx33 PC or a Mac with 68030 processor. And make sure your computer has at least 8Mb of RAM (that's 8 megabites of Random Access Memory). There - gabble over! You can open your eyes again now.

> Action: BoTom smiles reassuringly. Don't despair if you can't get hold of a powerful PC or mega Mac. The good news is you can still use all sorts of neat Net stuff like e-mail with just about any computer. ;-)

<The service provider>

> If you've read WhatistheInternet?@page12, you'll already know the Net is held together by powerful

e-mail //e-mail@page33
newsgroups //Newsgroups@page64
browser //WWW@page43
Action //IRC@page79

computers that are permanently connected to each other. In order to get on-line you have to link your 'pooter up to one of these machines. Well, that's where the service provider (or Internet access provider, as they are sometimes known) comes in.

> Service providers are companies which allow you to use their computers to connect to the Net – for a fee, of course! There are now hundreds of service providers and no matter where you live there will be at least one covering your area. You'll find an up-to-the-minute list of service providers in the back of many Internet magazines.

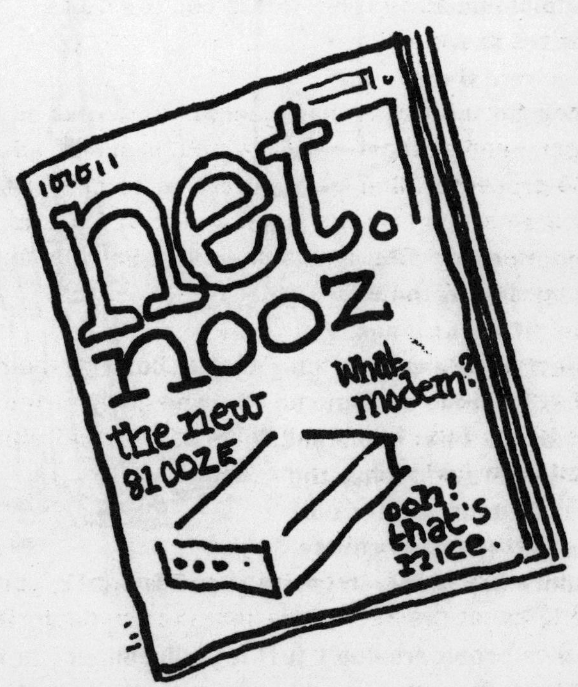

> BoTip
> If you're choosing a service provider, make sure you pick one with a POP (point of presence) nearby. This means that the number your compooter dials to connect to the service provider is a local number. Otherwise, your phone bill (and your parents) will go through the roof!

> Service providers can connect you to the Net in different ways. You can just have e-mail or go for full Internet access. It depends on what you want to do on-line and what the power of your 'pooter will allow you to do. Of course, the more you want, the more it costs. $-(

> Service providers don't just let you connect to their machines. They also provide you with all the software

your computer needs to make the connection. Usually you get a package of programs which includes a selection of Net tools such as e-mail, a newsreader and a browser.

> Some service providers offer even more. As well as connecting you to the Net, they give you access to their own private networks. These service providers are called on-line services and include companies like CompuServe and America On Line. Their private networks are very easy to use with lots of interesting places to go. The downside is that they tend to be more X-pensive and some cannot give you full access to the Net.

<The modem>

> In order to link your computer to the service provider you will need a modem. This is a device that allows computers to exchange information via a phone line.

> Ready for *another* bit of techno-gabble? The name <<modem>> comes from modulator demodulator. That's what a modem does; it modulates (converts digital information computers can understand into sound signals which can be sent down a phone line) and demodulates (translates sound signals back into digital information). OK, you can look now!

> You can get internal modems, which fit inside your computer, or external modems, which – you guessed it – are external. Who said hoomans weren't logical? It doesn't really matter which kind you use. What does make a difference, though, is the speed of your modem.

> A modem's speed is usually measured in bps. This refers to the number of bits per second it can transmit (a bit is the basic unit of computer data). The bigger this number, the better, because you'll have to wait less time while your computer downloads or sends information.

> If you are thinking of doing some serious surfing on the Net a 14,400 bps modem is the minimum you'll need. If you're just using e-mail you can get away with a less powerful model.

> BoTip
> It's a good idea to ask your service provider about the speed of the modem at their end. There's no point in forking out for a modem that's phaster than your service provider's modem, or the service provider will just slow you down. If you find out that your service provider's modem is a real slug, the solution is simple - find another service provider!

> *yawn* :-0

> Finished at last.

>That just about covers everything you'll need to blast into cyberspace. But what if you haven't got your own computer or a modem? Don't worry - meet me for a cup of hot chocolate at a cybercafe in //Nocomputer?@page31.

> Logoff.

surfing //WWW@page42
e-mail //e-mail@page33
cyberspace //Netspeak@page 95

Emoticons

> BoTom's back on-line!

> Just because we can only type on the Net, it doesn't mean we don't have feelings. Add a bit of e-motion to your Net life - all you need are emoticons (emotion + icon). If you can't make out what they are supposed to be, try looking at them sideways!

> There are *zillions* of these cute little characters. Here's one of my favourites:

{:-<))

>Do you know what it is?
>A sad man with a double chin, wearing a wig, of course!

:-)	happy
:-(	sad
:->	very happy
:-<	terribly sad
:-D	laughing
:'-(	crying
X-(	dead
:-P	sticking tongue out
:-0	yawn
B-)	wearing glasses
:-*	kiss
?:-o	surprise
{}	hug
;-)	wink
:-X	saying nothing
$-)	greedy
{hmmm}00oo.. :-/	thinking

>You will come across lots more and maybe even make up some of your own.

> See ya (but I wouldn't want to be ya). Bye!

No computer? No problem!

> Login.

> If you've read //What-u-need@page21, you'll know that to get on-line you've got to have a computer, a modem and an account with a service provider. But what if you haven't got these things? Does it mean *SYSTEM ERROR!* you can't get on the Net? :'-(

> *No!* :-)

> Don't worry. Lots of regular Net users don't have their own computer. How do they manage? Easy – they borrow someone else's. There are loads of places where you can get on the Net. And some are free!

> Think about school. Go on force yourself! More and more schools are going on-line. If there's a computer club at your school, find out if they have access to the Net. If they have – join it quick! If not, tell them about all the amazing things students could discover using the Net.

Tell them how they could use it like an encyclopedia to look up phacts and inphormation and link up with schools in other countries. Try to catch your teachers off guard by bombarding them with enth-oo-siasm. And, remember, do your shoelaces up. Good luck.

> And what about libraries? <<But they are full of books and people in cardigans>> I hear you say. Nonsense. Loads and I mean *LOADS* of libraries now have computers. And lots are on the Net! In fact, by 1998 there should be one computer connected to the Net in every single public library in the land. Better still, libraries are a super-cheap way to surf. Many let children use the Net for *free* and there's always someone to offer advice and help you. Even if they are wearing a cardigan.

> Cybercafes are popping up everywhere you look. You'll find them in cities from Brighton to Edinburgh. On each table (next to the sugar and serviettes) there's a computer. When you order your cakes and buns you can also buy half an hour or so surfing on the Net. What a phantastic idea! And because you're surrounded by other surfers, help is always at hand if you get stuck. It's not too expensive either: prices start at just £1.50 for half an hour (but chocolate cake is extra!).

> All universities are on the Net and most actually encourage people in the local community (that's you!) to come and use their facilities. The computers at universities are usually connected permanently to the Net. This means it doesn't cost them any extra money to let you have a go because they are always on-line anyway. Call up the computer department and see what's on offer. The holidays are a specially good time to try because all the stoodents have gone home.

> Talk to your family. If one of them works for a company, there's a good chance that the firm is on-line. Ask them to check. If it is, get them to talk to whoever is in charge. Maybe you could pop in one afternoon and the system controller could give you a surfing lesson. All it would cost the company is the price of a local phone call to their service provider. That's not much to ask!

> More and more places are going on-line. No matter where you live there will be somewhere you can get on the Net at a price you can afford. Keep searching till you find it.

> Logoff

e-mail

> BAK

> Stamps. They make a smashing collection. Lousy way of sending messages though! Apart from the fact that snail mail can take days – even weeks – to arrive, there's another far bigger problem. Stamps taste DISGUSTING! It's like sellotaping your tongue to a Brussels sprout. You'd have thought by now that someone would have invented chocolate flavoured stamps. They haven't. They invented e-mail instead. And when it comes to sending messages, e-mail can't be licked. Can't be licked – geddit? *ROTFL*

BAK //TLA@page63
ROTFL //TLA@page63

> e-mail is wonderful. And don't just take a humble bot's word for it. (Did I say humble?) It's a phact, e-mail is the most widely used tool on the whole of the Internet. Millions of messages are delivered every single day.

> Most service providers include an e-mail package in the start-up software they give you when you join the Net. If you didn't get one or fancy trying a new program - no problem! Nip over to the Virtual Shopping Trolley for details of where you can download some *cool* e-mail software.

> e-mail stands for electronic mail (you knew that). It allows you to post messages to other compooters anywhere in the world. All you do is type what you want to say, press a button and your message is sent instantly just round the corner or right across the world.

> Like snail mail, e-mail needs the correct address so the electronic postman can send your message to the right place. Addresses for e-mail look confusing. Don't panic. Once you know what each part stands for, they are easy to understand.

> A typical e-mail address looks like this:

doreen@fred.netulike.co.uk

> Let me explain how it works . . .

> BoTip

> Stop. Or rather don't stop. Full stop that is. What I'm trying to say is, don't put full stops at the end of e-mail addresses. It's a common mistake but it causes all sorts of problems. And don't use capital letters either!

doreen	The name or nickname of the user. In your e-mail address the first word will be whatever you've decided to call yourself.
@	Means <<at>>.
fred	The name of the computer to which the e-mail is being sent. Doreen calls her computer Fred!
netulike	This is the name of Doreen's <<service provider>>, the company that owns the host computer which connects her to the Internet.
co	This is the type of organisation that the service provider's computer belongs to. In this case <<c o>> stands for a company.
uk	Tells you which country the host computer is in.

> So, from her e-mail address, we know that Doreen uses a computer called Fred which is connected to the Net through Netulike, which is a company in the UK. See, told you it was easy!

> Here's a list of other codes and what kind of organisations they represent:

edu	School or college, except UK educational institutions, which use <<a c>>.
com	Company, except UK companies, which use <<co>>.
gov	Government organisation.
mil	Military establishment – err, like the army!
org	An organisation (such as a charity or the BBC).

> Every country has its own code too. There are at least 140 countries on the Net. Here's just a short selection to aid you in your Net detective work:

au	Australia
ca	Canada
de	Germany
jp	Japan
se	Sweden

> Computers in America don't have a country code at the end of their e-mail addresses. So, if you see a blank where the country code should be you know it's from the USA. Here's a good example:

<<president@whitehouse.gov>>

Yes – you can e-mail the president of the United States! Translated, the address reads: The President at the White House which is a government organisation in (because there's no country code) America.

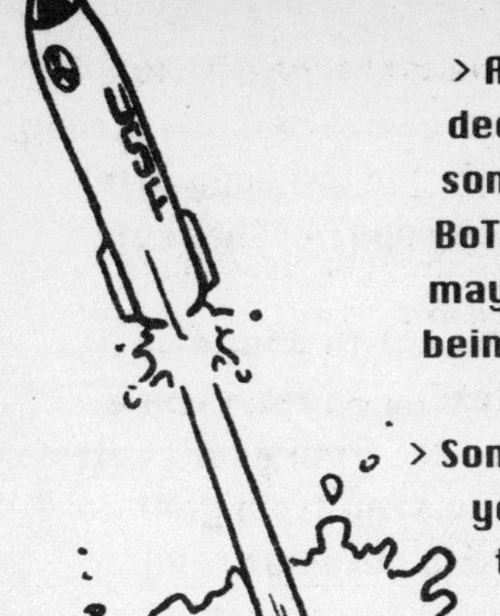

> And remember, if you do decide to send the President some e-mail, say hello from BoTom. On second thoughts, maybe not. He might think you're being cheeky and call in the CIA.

> Someone's e-mail address is all you need to start sending them messages. So go into your mail client and open up a new document. The top should look something like this:

To:
From:
Subject:
CC:
BCC:
Attachments:

> Put the e-mail address of the person you are writing to where it says <<To:>>. Your own e-mail address will appear automatically after the word <<From:>>. Now write a short description of what you are writing about in the line after <<subject:>>. If you send more than one e-mail to the same person this allows them to work out which is which without opening them all up.

> You can also send a <<CC>> (carbon copy - an identical copy) of your e-mail to other people. Just put the e-mail address of the person you want to send it to

client //Netspeak@page94

after <<CC:>>. Or, if you don't want the person to whom the e-mail is addressed to know you're sending a copy to someone else, put the address for the copy after <<BCC:>>. This is a <<blind carbon copy>>. *Sneaky!*

> Finally, you can add an attachment to your e-mail. This could be anything – a picture, a photo, even a game! Just choose <<Attach file>> from your control bar, select the thing you want to send from your hard drive and the name of the file will automatically appear after <<Attachments:>>.

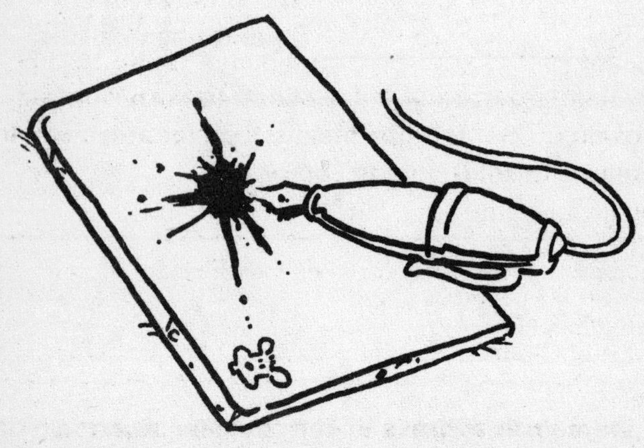

> But how do you add that extra personal touch to your e-mail? With a signature of course! Obviously you can't use your own handwriting. Signatures on the Net mean something slightly different – but they're just as individual.

> A sig (to use the Netspeak word) is your own unique way of signing off. You can use it on e-mail and in

newsgroups at the end of your mailings. Usually it includes your name and nick, snail mail address and/or telephone number. Some sigs include a short snappy sentence, for example:

Kate Kelland
199 Alderny St London SE21 0XX
<<My other computer is an Apple Mac>>

These are the car-bumper stickers of the Internet. The furry dice come in the form of ASCII art. These are pictures created using just characters on the keyboard. Only plain text characters are allowed (plain text is also called American Standard Code for Information Interchange - ASCII). This means the signature can be decoded by absolutely any compooter.

```
Francesca Stich <<call me Cuddles>>     {._.}
27a St James Street                     /(•)\
Manchester                              () ()
```

> The starship Enterprise is very popular signature. (Don't ask me why!)

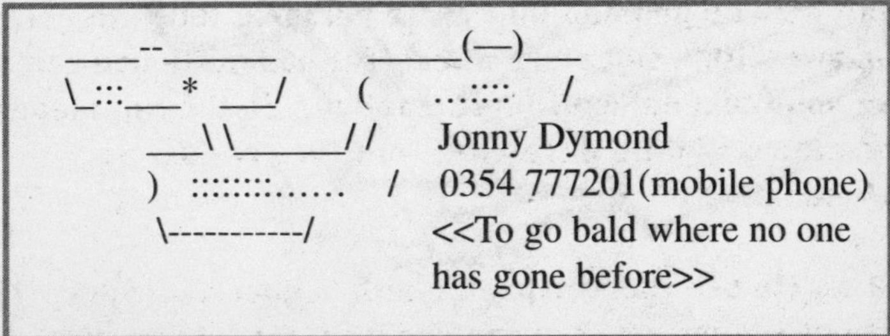

nick //IRC@page76 and //Netspeak@page96

> Making up your own sig is a must. But be warned, it's considered bad manners to have a signature that's over five full lines long. Huge sigs waste bandwidth and other users won't thank you if they have to download a gigabit of ASCII art every time you send them a message. Keep your sigs short and snappy!

> Once you've composed your sig, save it under the «Signature» option in your mail software. If you want, you can adjust your mail preferences so that your sig appears on all the mail you send.

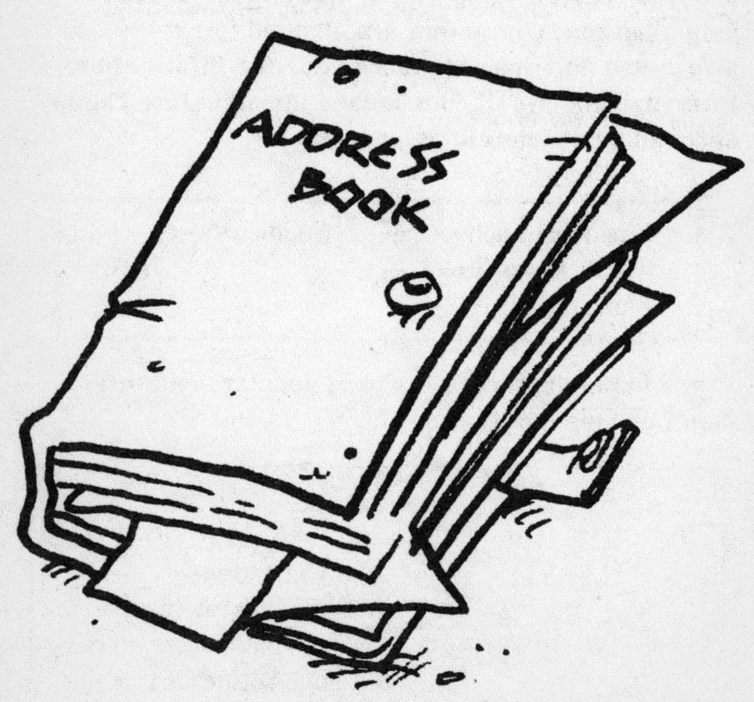

> As well as sending mail, you'll receive loads. To reply to a mailing just select <<REPLY>> from the control bar. A new e-mail page will appear with <<To:>> already filled in with the correct e-mail address.

> You won't have to be on the Net long before you've got loads of keypals. To save you typing in their address every time you send them e-mail, you can create an address book.

> When you want to send a letter to someone in your address book, just open it up and double-click on your pal's name. A new e-mail document with the correct address filled in at the top will appear instantly. *Smile!*

> That's all for now!

> Yours sincerely,

```
   ___
 /     \
{---(O)-(O)
 |    U  |
  ( \_/ ) BoTom
   ~~~~~
```

bad manners //Netiquette@page18
bandwidth //Netspeak@page94
keypals //Netspeak@page95

World Wide Web

> The Bot is back!

> Ooooh happiness! This chapter is all about surfing. It's my favourite activity. Worried that the salt water will ruin your keyboard or that your folks might notice the ironing board is missing? Don't be. Just grab your cyber-swimming trunks and follow me as we go in search of virtual waves...

> Surfing, as we all know, is Netspeak for <<exploring the World Wide Web>> (or <<the Web>> as it's known for short, <<WWW>> as it's known for shorter or just <<3W>>

as it's known for shortest). Whatever you call it, the Web is wonderful. Everything that's anything is on the Web with pictures, sounds, cartoons and video. You can surf through museums and look at their exhibits, visit pop groups and hear their latest songs, look stuff up in encyclopedias, play games, read magazines – I could go on and on!

> In fact, I will go on and on. And on! For a list of my favourite hot spots on the Web and where to find them, nip over to //WWW.BoTspots@page53.

> In order to find your way around the Web, you need a browser. This is a nifty piece of software that allows you to move from one Web site to another just by clicking your mouse. The reason why the Web is so popular is that browsers are so easy to use. The only downside is that you need a fairly powerful computer to use one.

> There are loads of different browsers to choose from. You'll find a selection in my Virtual Shopping Trolley.

> Once you've got a browser sorted out, you're ready to surf. The Web is made up of thousands and thousands of different sites. Each site can have hundreds of pages and be connected to lots of other sites and pages. So how do you find your way around?

> There are three different ways to get to a Web site.

powerful computer //What-u-need@page21
Virtual Shopping Trolley //VirtualShoppingTrolley@page81

> If you know the address of the Web page that you want to visit, you can type it in the browser's location window and press <<RETURN>>. A typical address looks like this:

http://www.public.iastate.edu/~entomology/InsectAsFood.html

> Don't be put off because the addresses look like gobbledygook. They're easy to understand, once you know how:

http://	HyperText Transfer Protocol - the language used to send information around the Web. This tells you that this is an address on the Web.
www.public.iastate.edu	This tells you all about the computer the Web page is on. This is one that the public have access to in Iowa State University, an educational organisation in America. This part of the URL works just like an e-mail address.
~entomology	This is the name of a directory inside the computer. Listed in it will be the file that contains the Webb page.
InsectAsFood.html	This is the name of the file we need to open in order to access the Web page. This particular page explains all about using insects as food and includes recipes for chocolate-chip cookies with grasshoppers. Yum!

URL //Netspeak@page96
e-mail address //e-mail@page34

> Well, that's fine if you know the address of the page you want to visit. What if you don't? No problem! :-> You can use a search engine to find it for you. Search engines are a bit like virtual librarians. You simply tell them what you're looking for and they see if they can find it for you. There's a list telling you where to find some of the better ones in: //WWW.BoTspots@page53.

> Let me explain how it works. Suppose you wanted to teach yourself to speak Klingon (the language spoken by some of the aliens in Star Trek). Use your browser to go to a search engine. Then enter the word (or words) you want to look up - in this case <<Klingon>>. After a few seconds, a list of Web sites that feature the word will appear, together with a description of what each site is about.

> If you see what you're looking for, double-click on the address and you'll automatically go there. If no pages look any good, try entering another word or using another search engine.

> Oh, and in case you really do want to learn to speak Klingon, just go to the Klingon Language Institute at:

http://www.kli.org/klihome.html

BoTip

Picking the word you want the search engine to look up takes a bit of skill. If you enter a word that's really general (such as <<kids>>) you'll end up with thousands of suggestions you'll never be able to read. <u>OTOH</u>, if you are too specific, you might miss the thing you're looking for. You'll just have to experiment. Don't give up. Whatever you're looking for, it's out there somewhere!

> OK so far? :-) Don't worry - the rest is easy!

> When you're in a Web page you'll notice some words are highlighted (usually underlined or in blue, although you can make it any colour you like). These are hypertext links. They are the third way of getting around. And they are what makes the Web so special!

> You can move to a new Web page simply by clicking on a highlighted word. For example, suppose you are reading an article about whales in your favourite <u>e-zine</u> and you come across the sentence <<...and the environmental organisation Greenpeace has been

OTOH //TLA@page63
e-zine //Netspeak@page95

campaigning to ban all whale hunting...>>. Simply clicking on the highlighted word <<Greenpeace>> will zip you off to another Web page where you can learn more about these eco-warriors.

>It works just like the hypertext links in this book, by taking you to pages where there's something you might need to know.

> With hypertext links you can forget all about URL addresses. You just click on any highlighted word that takes your fancy and nose your way around the Web according to what looks interesting. *WOW* Cool, huh?

> It's a doddle. Even adults who still can't work out how to program the video recorder can use hypertext. So it must be easy! Just click on the links you want to follow and you'll bounce from one Web page to another on a computer thousands of miles away - all in a matter of seconds!

> You can keep on following hypertext links forever. But, of course, having clicked on a link and gone to a page, you may want to go back to where you were. Easy! Just click the <<BACK>> button on your browser's control panel and you'll return to the previous Web page . . .

> And when you return, you'll notice that the hypertext link you clicked on has changed colour (usually to purple or red – but again you can set it to any colour you like, using your browser's <<OPTIONS>> settings). This enables you to keep track of where you've been so you don't keep visiting the same sites.

> Your browser will be packed with useful functions like this. If it's not, get another browser! Let me go over what some of the other main control buttons do.

<<FORWARD>>

> While you are surfing, your computer remembers the

Web pages you visit and stores them in its memory. Suppose you click on a hypertext link, then click the «BACK» button. You're back where you started. But if you want to have another look at the page you just saw, click the «FORWARD» button. You could simply click the hypertext link again – but that would mean waiting while your computer downloaded the page for a second time. Clicking the «FORWARD» button calls the page up from memory and allows you to view it instantly.

«HOME»

> This takes you back to your home page. You can set your home page to be any page you like on the Web. Lots of people choose their favourite search engine. That way, just by clicking on this button, they can return to the searcher to look something up. The home page is also the page your browser goes to automatically when you connect to the Web. It will be the starting point for every journey you make on the Web.

«STOP»

> If you start downloading a page, but change your mind and decide to go somewhere else just click «STOP» to cancel the operation.

«NEW WINDOW»

> You can look at several different Web pages all at once – provided, of course, your computer has got enough memory. This is particularly useful when you're waiting for something to download. Don't hang around! Simply open up a new window and carry on exploring.

downloading //VirtualShoppingTrolley@page85

<<SEARCH>>

> Browsers usually come with their own search engine. Again you just type in a key word and wait for a list of suggested Web sites to pop up. You'll find it useful but not as powerful as some of the other search tools.

<<BOOKMARK>>

> This is dead useful! You're bound to find lots of Web sites that you'll want to go back to again and again. Well, instead of typing in their <u>URL</u> address each time or using a search engine, just go to the site and make a bookmark. Now, the next time you want to visit the site, click on the Bookmarks menu and select the one you want. Your browser will do the rest!

<<IMAGES>>

> This allows you to choose whether or not your browser automatically downloads the pictures included on a Web page. If you turn the images off, pictures will appear as little icons and you can choose whether or not to look at them. Just click your mouse on any you do want to see. Pages will download faster if the images are turned off. The disadvantage is . . . you won't see the pictures!

> Time for a tea break.

> (_)D Ahhhh! Lovely cuppa.

> That's better. Now where was I? Oh, yes – pictures...

> If you see a picture you really like, why not download it into your computer permanently? That way you can print it out or use it as your computer's start-up screen. It's a cinch. Let me show you how it's done.

> First click on the picture. This will call up the full image – often Web pages just show you part of a picture or a shrunken version. Now choose <<SAVE THIS IMAGE>> from your <<FILE>> menu. With some browsers you can just click on the image again. Give the picture a name and chose where to put it on your hard disk, then press <<RETURN>>. *Bingo!* It's yours.

> And it's not just pictures you can download and keep. You can copy sounds, animations and videos on to your hard disk too. When one of these is up for grabs, you'll

see some kind of icon. Just double-click on it and you'll start downloading.

> Sounds easy. And it is! But before you begin downloading sounds and movies, make sure you've got all the software you need to hear and watch them. Otherwise it's a bit pointless! You can get everything you need quite easily. For more details check out the Virtual Shopping Trolley (VST).

> And another thing! Some of the files you download may have been compressed so they will download faster. You will need to expand the files before you can run the program and this also requires special software. Never fear – my VST comes to the rescue again!

> Now the only thing left to do is take the plunge – and surf!

> By the way, if you're still hopelessly confused, there's loads of free advice on the Web about how to use it. You'll find the addresses of some friendly help sites, as well as other cool places to go, in //WWW.BoTspots@page53.

> BFN!

Virtual Shopping Trolley //VirtualShoppingTrolley@page85
BFN //TLA@page63

//WWW.BoTspots

> The World Wide Web is a big place. If you're feeling lost, don't worry! Let me show you around. Come with me on a tour of some of my favourite sites where you can find everything from games to goldfish!

http://wwwnpac.syr.edu/textbook/kidsweb

Kidsweb. A great starting point on the Web with useful links to loads of other top sites.

http://www.kidlink.org/

Make some virtual friends. Check out the brilliant Kidlink site to discover about kids-only IRC, and how to get a keypal.

http://www.metawire.com/stars/

Seeing stars! Read your horoscope here and see what the future may have in store!

IRC //IRC@page74

http://legowww.homepages.com/

Mindbending models. The Lego home page is well worth a look.

http://gagme.wwa.com/~boba/kidsi.html

Thanks Uncle Bob! A huge selection of interesting sites for kids, handpicked by <<Uncle Bob>>.

http://www.ot.com:80/kids/

Kids corner. A cool site with puzzles, games and an interactive adventure.

http://www.nhm.ac.uk/

Make an exhibition of yourself at the Natural History Museum, where else?

http://www.digimark.net/TheSimpsons/

Eat my shorts! If you love Bart Simpson, this is the place to come.

http://postcards.www.media.mit.edu/postcards/

Wish you were here? Send someone a postcard via e-mail. What a brilliant idea!

http://wwwtios.cs.utwente.nl/say/

Back chat. Type in a word and your computer will say it back you!

http://robotO.ge.uiuc.edu/~carlosp/color/

Art attack. Create your own pictures using a virtual colouring book.

http://www.gamesdomain.co.uk

Games galore! Reviews, cheats and games you can download - it's all here!

http://www.yahoo.com/Recreation/Games/Internet_Games/Interactive_Web_Games/

Play away! Stacks of interactive games you can play against a human or a bot opponent.

http://manor.york.ac.uk/htdocs/bships.html

Battle stations! Play a game of battleships against a bot.

http://lycos.cs.cmu.edu/

Seek it out. Lycos is a really useful search engine to help you hunt out what you're looking for on the Web.

http://www.yahoo.com

Can't find what you're looking for? Try searching for it using Yahoo.

http://www.willamette.edu./~tjones/chessmain.html

Check it out. Fancy a game of chess? Then this is the place to be!

http://kilp.media.mit.edu:8001/power/home.html

Go! Go! Power Ranger fans. Loads of info on these teen-superheroes, plus great pictures to download.

http://cool.infi.net/

What's cool? This is! A list of the best sites to visit on the Web.

http://www.en-garde.com/kidpub/

Write on! Read stories written by other kids and leave a story that YOU have written.

http://einstein.et.tudelft.nl/~arlet/slide.cgi

Slidey puzzle. A cute little puzzle that's guaranteed to drive you bonkers!

http://www.woodwind.com:80/cyberkids/

Hot off the press: A fanastic e-zine for kids with games, puzzles, jokes and stories.

http://www2.netscape.com/fishcam/fishcam.html

Something fishy is going on! See for yourself - live video clips of the inside of someone's fish tank!

http://rrws6.wiwi.uni-regensburg.de/SONNENSTEIN/sonnenstein.html

To the rescue! Interactive on-line adventure in which YOU are the hero.

http://iquest.com/~pinnacle/index.html

Work it out! Puzzles, puzzles and more puzzles!

http://www.rl.af.mil:8001/Odds-n-Ends/sbcam/rlsbcam.html

Snow joke! Try throwing a virtual snowball!

http://rs6000.bvis.uic.edu:80/museum/Dna_To_Dinosaurs.html

Dino-mite! An amazing virtual museum that explores the prehistoric world of the dinosaurs.

http://www.bev.net/education/SeaWorld/homepage.html

Animal magic. Games, puzzles and stacks of extraordinary info on all sorts of amazing animals.

http://www.batcon.org

Bat Conservation International. Loads of info about bats.

http://buildacard.com/

How crafty! Design your own greetings card and send it by e-mail to a friend.

http://www.cs.ubc.ca/spider/jwu/origami.html

Fold on! How to make amazing models out of paper.

http://arachnid.cs.cf.ac.uk/htbin/RobH/hangman

Don't hang about. Play hangman instead.

http://scitech.lm.com/

Fancy a walk? Then take a stroll along a virtual nature trail.

http://fermi.clas.virginia.edu/~gl8f/pbm_links.html

Game on! A huge list of FREE games you can play, using e-mail.

http://studl.tuwien.ac.at/~e8826423/LemmGames.html

Roll up, roll up! Get your free Lemmings demos here!

TLAs & ETLAs

>HELLO (Hi Everybody! Let's Log On.)

> It's time we had a word about acronyms and abbreviations. Everyone on the Net is potty about them, especially in IRC.

> An acronym is a word made up out of the first letter of each word in a group of words, like SCUBA (self-contained underwater breathing apparatus).

> In RL we often use abbreviations such as BBC (British Broadcasting Corporation) or VIP (very important person).

> On the Net, you'll find acronyms and abbreviations everywhere! I've already used two abbreviations in the last few lines, IRC (Internet Relay Chat) and RL (real life). You see I just can't stop myself!

> Both acronyms and abbreviations are known as TLAs and they are always written in capital letters. The name TLA stands for <<three- (or sometimes two-) letter acronym/abbreviation>>.

> As well as TLAs, there are ETLAs (extended three-letter acronyms/abbreviations). In other words, three-letter acronyms/abbreviations with more than three letters!

> Opposite are some of the TLAs and ETLAs you're likely to encounter.

AFAIK	As far as I know
AFK	Away from keyboard
AOL	America On Line
BAK	Back at keyboard
BBL	Be back later
BFN	Bye for now
BRB	Be right back
BTW	By the way
FB	Furrowed brow (angry!)
GAL	Get a life
GOTO	Go to
GTRM	Going to read mail
HAND	Have a nice day
HTH	Hope this helps
IMO	In my opinion
IMHO	In my humble opinion (Creep!)
IOW	In other words
IRC	Internet Relay Chat
L8R	Later
LOL	Laugh out loud (or lots of laughs)
NRN	No reply necessary (often attached to e-mail or articles in newsgroups)
OIC	Oh I see
OTOH	On the other hand
RL	Real life (as opposed to life on the Net)
ROTFL	Roll on the floor laughing (funnier than LOL)
RTM	Read the manual (this one is for you newbies!)
SOL	Sooner or later
SWIM?	See what I mean?
SYL	See you later
TTYL	Talk to you later

If you see any you can't work out for yourself, don't be afraid to ask what they mean.

America On Line //What-u-need@page25
newbies //Netspeak@page96

Newsgroups

> So what is it you want to know? I don't just mean about newsgroups. Anything at all! Go on, think of something you always wondered about. What's the currency of Albania? Why do stars twinkle? Are your neighbours really aliens? No matter what your burning question is, you can bet you'll find the answer on <<Usenet>>.

> Usenet works like a bulletin-board – a sort of computerised notice-board. Anyone with access to Usenet can pin a message to the board and read all the messages left there by other people. What's more, by replying to other people's messages, you can get discussions going!

> The good thing about Usenet is you don't need a powerful machine to get on it. Almost any computer will do – you just need to get hold of some software that will allow you to read and post messages. Some Web browsers will let you do this, but there are programs called <<newsreaders>> which are especially designed for the job. If you don't have one already,

bulletin-board //WhatistheInternet?@page14
browsers //WWW@page43
VST //VirtualShoppingTrolley@page84

there's a selection in the UST, just waiting to be downloaded.

> Of course there's one big difference between this and other notice-boards. Around 30 million people can use Usenet! And that can lead to an awful lot of messages – roughly 100,000 new ones every single day! This is why messages are put into categories called «newsgroups».

> Each newsgroup has its own topic. There are 15,000 different newsgroups covering every subject you could ever think of: comics, games, life on Mars, pets, practical jokes, ASCII art. The list is endless! Here are a few of my favourites:

alt.tv.simpsons	Everything you ever wanted to know about The Simpsons.
alt.kids-talk.penpals	Looking for an Internet penpal to send e-mail to? Then look no further!
alt.shenanigans	A newsgroup for practical jokers to swap ideas for perfect pranks.
rec.pets.cats	If you're a cat-lover, then this is the purrfect place for you!
comp.sys.ibm.pc.games	The vast list of newsgroups for PC games fans starts here.
news.newusers.questions	All the answers to common newbie questions about the Net.
alt.cybercafes	Find out about your nearest cybercafe.

> With so many newsgroups to choose from, how are you ever going find the ones you're interested in? Especially if you're the sort of person who can't find their socks on a Monday morning! No problem, it's easy! ;-)

ASCII //e-mail@page39 and Netspeak@94
cybercafe //No computer?@page31

> Think of newsgroups as leaves on a tree. Each leaf has its own address telling you exactly where on the tree you can find it. All you have to do is follow the directions along the branches and twigs. Take a look at a typical newsgroup address:

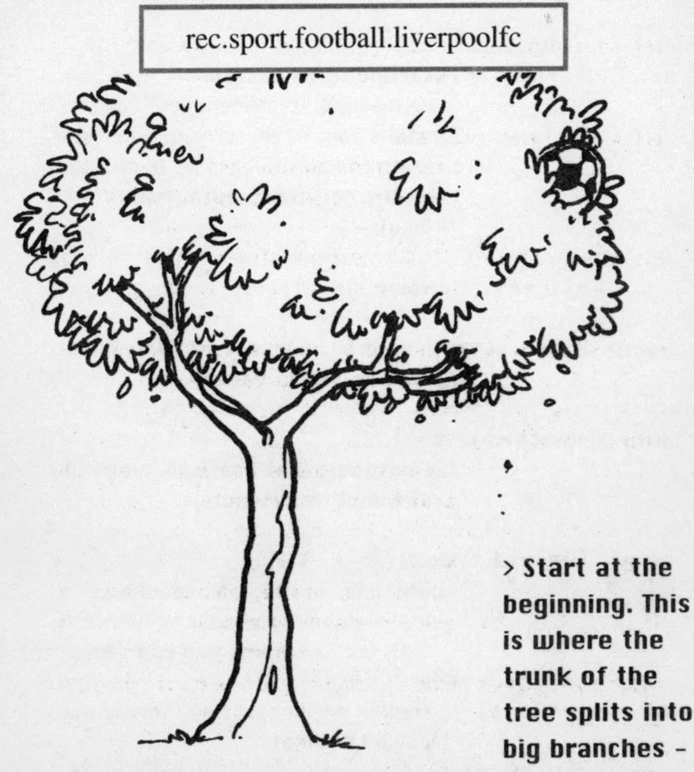

> Start at the beginning. This is where the trunk of the tree splits into big branches – you want the one called <<rec>> which has to do with recreation and hobbies. Select it with a click of the mouse and you'll see this branch splits up into several smaller branches. In this case you want to open up <<sport>>. Now you're getting down to the twigs. Click on the one called <<football>>. Finally, pick your leaf

<<liverpoolfc>> where you'll find postings about Liverpool Football Club. See, it's easy!

> When you're exploring, the trick is to pick the right big branch! Here's a list of just a few.

alt. (alternative)	There's some fun stuff in here but, be warned, it's a hang-out for weird adults too. If you or your folks are worried about what you might find on the Net, check out //Adults Only!@10.
biz. (business)	Yawn :-O
comp. (computers)	Loads of excellent info on games here in <<comp.games>>.
misc. (miscellaneous)	Everything that doesn't fit into any of the other categories.
news. (Usenet itself)	Great for getting advice on how to use a new newsreader or where to look for something you can't find.
talk. (debates)	Feeling argumentative? This is the place to come!
uk. (United Kingdom)	Anything to do with the UK, from politics to what's on telly.

> Once you've found an interesting newsgroup, before you do anything else, have a look at the file called

<<F A Q>> (frequently asked questions). Every newsgroup has one. It explains what the newsgroup is about and answers the questions most people ask when they first arrive. Ignore the FAQs and you risk getting flamed for asking silly questions.

> Next to all the articles in the newsgroup, you'll see a few words describing what each posting is about and a number indicating how many people have added replies. To have a look at something just click on it with your mouse. When you close it again you'll see the article now has a little tick or dot in front of it to remind you that you've already seen it.

>If you'd like to reply to something you're reading, just choose

flamed //Netspeak@page95

the <<REPLY>> button from the control bar in your newsreader. A document will pop up for you to type in. Write your reply, then click <<SEND>>. You may also have the option of sending a reply direct to the person's e-mail address.

>BoTip
> Messages are deleted from newsgroups when they are three or four days old. People may find themselves reading your reply without being able to read the

original posting. So it's a good idea to copy and paste the relevant part of the original posting at the top of your reply. Put << >> around the parts you've copied to show that you are quoting, and say who posted the original article. Let me show you:

> <<Does anyone know of a good cheat for DareDevil on the Mega Drive?>> writes Donna Endean.

> See what I mean? Now everyone who reads your reply will know what you are talking about.

> Of course, as well as posting replies to other people's articles, you may want to start a new discussion with an article of your own. This is called starting a <<thread>>. Simply select <<NEW THREAD>> from your control panel and type away!

> Before you send your posting, don't forget to add a short description of what your thread is about in the header at the top of the document. This will appear next to your article so people can decide if they want to download it to read what you have written.

> You may also want to add your signature before you post your article. Don't forget, long signatures are considered bad manners. So is writing in CAPITAL LETTERS. I beg your pardon - I don't know what came over me! For more details, check out the section on netiquette.

> Don't be surprised if your postings don't appear in the newsgroup the moment you send them. It will take a while for your news server to update its files.

> As we're on the subject of news servers, let me explain what they are. The way you access newsgroups using the Internet is to connect to a computer called a news server. The chances are that the service provider you use to get on-line is also a news server.

e-mail address //e-mail@page34
signature //e-mail@page38
netiquette //Netiquette@page18
server //Netspeak@page96
service provider //What-u-need@page22

> The news server has a vast database of Usenet articles and the newsgroups they appear in. No news server has every single newsgroup but many provide access to around 12,000. More than enough to keep you busy!

> All the Usenet news servers around the world are linked together in a chain. When you post a message, your news server doesn't just update its own database. It also sends a message along the chain telling the other computers to add your article to their databases. This means that what you've written can be read anywhere in the world!

> But it's not just people on the Net who can use Usenet. You can often access a number of newsgroups by connecting to local bulletin-boards – which are extremely cheap to join. Some satellite TV companies can provide you with a special decoder to connect to your computer. This allows you to read a huge selection of newsgroups but not to post your own messages.

> Finally, if you find there are some newsgroups that you visit all the time, why not subscribe to them? Just select the name of the newsgroup and click <<SUBSCRIBE>>. This way instead of having to look the newsgroup up, new articles will be sent to you automatically as soon as you open up your newsreader. Pretty neat huh?

> That is the end of the news. Good-night.

> Logoff.

IRC
(Internet Relay Chat)

>BoTom: Imagine, instead of ME doing the talking all the time, YOU could chip in now and again.

>Reader: What, you mean like this?

>BoTom: Oi! I said *imagine*. I didn't want you to actually start talking back. But I'm glad to see you've got the idea!

> Just wait till you get on IRC (Internet Relay Chat). Then you can have <<live>> conversations with other net users, except that, instead of speaking, you type what you want to say. Just as I've been doing!

> When you press <<RETURN>>, the text you've entered pops up on your screen and on the screens of all the people you're chatting with.

> IRC lets you have a conversation with lots of people who may be in different countries. You can chat to as many people as you like at the same time. Although, as in any other conversation, too many people talking at once can get confusing!

> To use IRC you need a reasonably powerful computer. If you can't surf the Web, I'm afraid your machine probably isn't up to the job. You'll also need an IRC

client (in other words a program that allows you to use IRC). It's unlikely your service provider will have included this software in your start-up pack but there's a selection of clients you can download (for free!) in my Virtual Shopping Trolley.

> When you use your IRC client, it will ask for the name of an IRC server (or it may suggest one you could try). The IRC server is the computer which links chattering Net users together. There are loads of servers including one that's just for kids. It's called Kidlink and you'll find everything you need to know at its Web site (the address is listed in //WWW.botspots@page53). Or you could try one of the hundreds of IRC servers listed in the newsgroup <<alt.IRC.>>.

service provider //What-u-need@page22
Virtual Shopping Trolley//VirtualShoppingTrolley@page85
server //Netspeak@page96
newsgroup//Newsgroups@page64

> When you connect to the server you'll have to choose a nick (your nickname). Your nick appears at the start of everything you say. At the beginning of this section, I gave you the nick <<Reader>>. But your nick can be anything – even Nick!

> Finally, once you've logged on to the server, you will need to join a channel. These are virtual rooms in cyberspace where people meet up for a natter. To find out which channels are available, simply type <</list>> and press <<RETURN>>.

> A list of all the channels will appear showing their name, the topic that's being discussed or a greeting, plus the number of people on the channel. The list will look a bit like this:

> **Friendly** <<friendly by name friendly by nature>> 18
> **Help!** <<advice for newbies from kind-hearted ops>> 3
> **Lonely** <no topic set> 1
> **Private** <<private>> 2
> **Teen** <<no adults allowed>> 5

> To join a channel, type <</join #channel name>> then press <<RETURN>>. So to join Teen, for example, you type <</join #Teen>>. A few seconds later a window will open – and you can start chatting!

> Don't be shy – introduce yourself! Type <<Hi!>> and press <<RETURN>>. You'll soon find out that IRC users are a very friendly bunch and there are lots of teen channels for kids.

> As well as joining other people's channels, you can set up your own. Once again, use the <</join #>> command, but this time invent a channel name. As long as that channel doesn't exist already, it will appear as a new channel with one person in it – you! Talking to yourself isn't much fun, so nip into another channel and ask if anyone wants to join you.

> If you're the person who set up the channel you become the channel operator. Being an op gives you special powers! Below is a list of useful IRC commands. Those on the second list can be performed only by ops.

>> On some of the commands, you have to type in details to replace what I have put in <<quotes>>. Simply fill in the details – but don't type the angle bracket quote marks!

/ignore <<nick>> * all	Blanks out anything said by <<nick>> on your screen.
/msg <<nick>> <<message>>	Sends a private message to <<nick>> which none of the other chatters can see.
/leave #<<channel name>>	To leave a channel.
/nick <<new nick>>	Changes your nickname.
/bye	Ends IRC session.

And now for those operator-only commands!

/topic <<topic>>	Changes the topic of the channel.
/kick <<nick>>	Boots <<nick>> off the channel. Bye!
/op <<nick>>	Makes <<nick>> an op too.

> To get a full list of commands, just type <</help>>. If you need more information about a specific command, type <</help>> followed by <<name of command>>. You'll be amazed at how easy it is! Soon you'll be chatting away to virtual phriends all over the world. You can swap e-mail addresses and become keypals too.

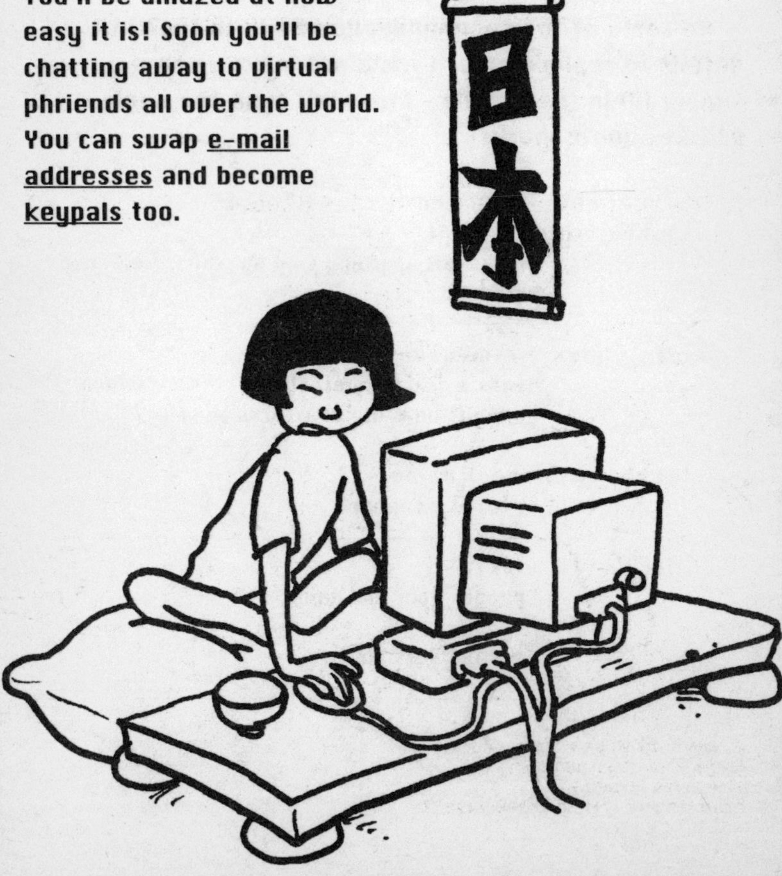

> The official language of IRC is netspeak. TLA and emoticons are used all the time. If you want to shout, use capital letters. LIKE THIS - OK? But don't do it too often or everyone will think you're a loud mouth! Because people are typing quickly as they chat, it's quite acceptable to make lots of spelling mistakes. It's far more important to keep the banter going than to worry about whether everything is spelt correctly.

> But people don't just talk on IRC. As well as chatting you can *do* things. These are called <<ACTIONS>>. They appear like this:

Action: BoT jumps up and down to grab everyone's attention!

> or...

Action: BoT sneaks up and tickles Reader!

e-mail address //e-mail@page34
keypals //Netspeak@page95
TLA //TLA@page61
emoticons //Emoticons@page27

> To perform an action just type <</ m e>> and then whatever it is you want to do. You don't need to type your nick. When you press <<RETURN>> your nick will appear automatically at the beginning of the action.

> That just about wraps it up for IRC except to say that humans aren't the only characters you'll bump into on IRC. There are lots of bots around too!

> We have all sorts of jobs. Some bots supervise or <<moderate>> channels - if you start swearing or being nasty to other chatterers we'll kick you out. Others are there to play games with humans. Bots can even chat to you. Sometimes it can be difficult working out who's a bot and who's not.

> Who knows, maybe you'll even bump into me!

Action: BoT disappears in a puff of smoke. Bye!

VIRTUAL SHOPPING TROLLEY

> Want some new Net software to help you cruise through cyberspace? Just step this way! All the programs you'll ever need on-line can be downloaded from the Internet. And some of it is *FREE!*

> If you're not sure how to download files, flick to the lowdown on downloading. But before you go, I have some advice you should read:

cyberspace //Netspeak@page95
downloading//downloading@page85

> When you start downloading stuff, the first thing you should get hold of is an up-to-date anti-virus program – just in case you download some infected files.

> Make sure you download a version of the software you want that is compatible with your machine. You won't get very far with the Apple Mac version of Netscape if you've got a PC with Windows!

> Most of the programs you'll download will be compressed. This allows them to be downloaded faster but you won't be able to use them until you expand them and this may require a special program. For example, PC files which end with «.zip» require a program called «WinZip» to open them; and for Mac files ending «.sit» you'll need «Stuffit». Some compressed files, however, are self-expanding – you just click on them and they open up. The addresses of this kind of file end with «.sea» which means self-extracting archive.

> Finally lots of software is freeware. This means it's yours to keep for ever and it doesn't cost a bean. But there is also shareware – and it's not the same thing! You don't have to pay to download shareware but it's not completely free either. The idea of shareware is that you can start using the program for nothing but if you like it and use it a lot, you are expected to send a small contribution to the person who created it. Sounds fair enough!

> OK lecture over! Now you can dive in and take your pick of the goodies on offer:

ANTI-VIRUS PROTECTION

Disinfectant (Mac - FREE!)
ftp://ftp.acns.nwu.edu/pub/disinfectant

F-Prot (PC - FREE!)
ftp://risc.ua.edu/pub/ibm-antivirus/

McAfee's Virus Scan (PC)
ftp://mcafee.com/pub/

BROWSERS

Netscape (PC or Mac)
ftp://src.doc.ic.ac.uk//packages/Netscape/

NCSA Mosaic (PC or Mac)
ftp:ftp.ncsa.uiuc.edu/Web/Mosaic

E-MAIL

Eudora Light (PC or Mac - FREE!)
ftp://ftp.qualcomm.com/quest/

Pegasus (PC - FREE!)
ftp://risc.ua.edu/pub/network/pegasus

COMPRESSION PROGRAMS

WinZip (PC)
ftp://ftp.WinZip.com/WinZip/

Stuffit (Mac)
ftp://ftp.aloha.net/pub/Mac/

NEWSREADERS

Free Agent (PC)
ftp://ftp.forteinc.com/pub/forte/free_agent/

Nuntius (Mac)
ftp://ftp.ruc.dk/pub/nuntius/

Newswatcher (Mac)
ftp://ftp.acns.nwu.edu/pub/newswatcher

FTP CLIENTS

WS-FTP (PC)
ftp://ftp.coast.net/SimTel/win3/winsock/

Anarchie (Mac)
ftp://ftp.share.com/pub/peterlewis/

IRC CLIENTS

Homer (Mac)
ftp://ftp.aloha.net/pub/Mac

mIRC (PC)
ftp://papa.indstate.edu/winsock-l/winirc/

MOVIE PLAYERS (for watching movies)

Sparkle
ftp://ftp.sunet.se:/pub/mac/info-mac/grf/util/

UMPeg (PC)
ftp://papa.indstate.edu/winsock-l/

SOUND PLAYERS (PC users require a sound card)

Sound App and Sound Machine (both Mac)
ftp://ftp.utexas.edu/pub/mac/sound/

The lowdown on downloading

> To download programs, you need an FTP <u>client</u>. The FTP stands for <<File Transfer Protocol>>, the language used by computers to exchange files. Sounds complicated. It

client //Netspeak@page94

isn't! Most browsers these days are also FTP clients. So you can do everything with the same tool you use to surf the Web.

>If you know the FTP address of the program you want to download, just type it into your browser as though you were typing in the address of a Web site. That's all there is to it! Press <<RETURN>> and you will go to the FTP site where you can download what you want simply by clicking on it.

If you don't know the FTP address, do a search for name of program you are looking for – just as if you were searching for a Web site. Your search engine will hunt down the software you're after and give you a hypertext link to the Web page it's on. Click on the link to go there and when you arrive, click on what you want to download. This will automatically take you to the right FTP address and start downloading.

It couldn't be easier . . . but it could be faster! That's why some Net users prefer dedicated FTP clients. These do the same thing as your Web browser but, because they are designed just for transferring files, they work faster. Your service provider may have given you an FTP client in your start-up software. If they haven't, don't worry – you can download one using your browser!

> FTP clients are easy to use. As with a browser, you simply enter the right FTP address and *bingo!* your FTP client will find it for you.

> And, if you don't know the address, you can look it

up. Most FTP clients also have their own special search engines that search for files you can download. The FTP client called Anarchie, for example, has a search program called Archie.

> So, suppose you want to download the latest version of Netscape using your FTP client. Open up «Anarchie», select «Archie», enter the word «Netscape», and a few minutes later Archie will report back with the addresses of all the versions of Netscape you can download. You just have to pick one and give the address to Anarchie.

> Now that wasn't too tricky, was it? But the best way to learn is to actually do it. So, come on, give it a go!

browsers //WWW@page43
searching for a Web site //WWW@page43
hypertext link //WWW@page46

BACK TO THE FUTURE

> Login.

> Why me? All the other Bots I know have nice easy jobs like sorting e-mail or playing games on IRC channels. But what do I end up doing? Explaining the Internet to hoomans, that's what. Typical!

> You see it's not that newbies are particularly thick. Well, not the younger ones anyway. It's just that the Net keeps on changing. Every time you look at it, it's grown even bigger and exciting new tools keep coming on-line. It simply refuses to stay still.

> The Net has been around for longer than you probably realise. Using the evidence of fossils (adults) we can trace the history of the Internet back to the prehistoric era of computing (the late 1960s). These were the days of dinosaur computers – vast machines so large that instead of sitting neatly on top of a desk they filled an entire room!

> Dinosaur computers suffered from all sorts of problems. For example, people now talk about <<bugs>> in a computer program, meaning a glitch or error. But originally, bugs were . . . bugs! Computers used to be so big that insects could crawl inside and cause them to go wrong. That's where the expression comes from.

e-mail //e-mail@page33
IRC //IRC@page74
newbies //Netspeak@page96

> Ah yes, those were the days. Anyway, as I was saying, that is when the Net began. It started with something called ARPANET (Advanced Research Projects Agency Network) - an American network which linked together top secret military computers.

> But why did the US army and secret service want a network of computers? To swap games of course! No, that's not the reason. Or at least not the main reason.

> The idea was that a complicated network of computers would be difficult for an enemy to destroy. Even if some of the computers were blown up in a war, the rest would still be able to send messages to each other through the undamaged links in the network. Pretty cunning, huh?

e-mail //e-mail@page33
newsgroups //Newsgroups@page64
FTP //VirtualShoppingTrolley@page85

> The next major development was in the 1970s when universities were allowed to link their computers to the ARPANET. This led to the invention of tools such as <u>e-mail</u>, <u>newsgroups</u> and <u>FTP</u>. What's more, when universities in Europe joined the system it meant the network had gone global!

> The number of computers on the ARPANET increased from 1,000 in 1983 to 60,000 in 1986. It was around this time that people started talking about the <<Internet>>. It was also around this time when they started <<talking>> on IRC!

> In 1991, companies were allowed to sell connections to the Internet. Now anyone could pay a service provider and go on-line - for the first time the Internet was open to the public! One year later the World Wide Web exploded on the scene and made surfing a cinch.

> But that's not the end of the story. The Net is *still* developing! For example, people have already started using Net phones. These turn your computer into a telephone, allowing you to call anywhere in the world - but instead of paying long-distance charges, you pay only for the local call to your service provider.

> The Web could also soon be transformed. In the not-too-distant future, sounds and animations will be activated immediately when you arrive at a Web page. No more hanging about, waiting for them to download into your computer! This also means you'll be able to watch whole movies as easily as putting a video in the VCR.

> But the biggest thing that's about to happen to the Net, is that millions more people like *YOU!* will soon join it. The bigger the Net gets, the better it will be. If it carries on expanding at the current rate, the Internet will soon become the most important and popular way of communication in the world. And you wouldn't want to miss out on that, would you?

IRC //IRC@page74
service provider //Netspeak@page££; and What-u-need@page96
World Wide Webb //WorldWideWebb@page42

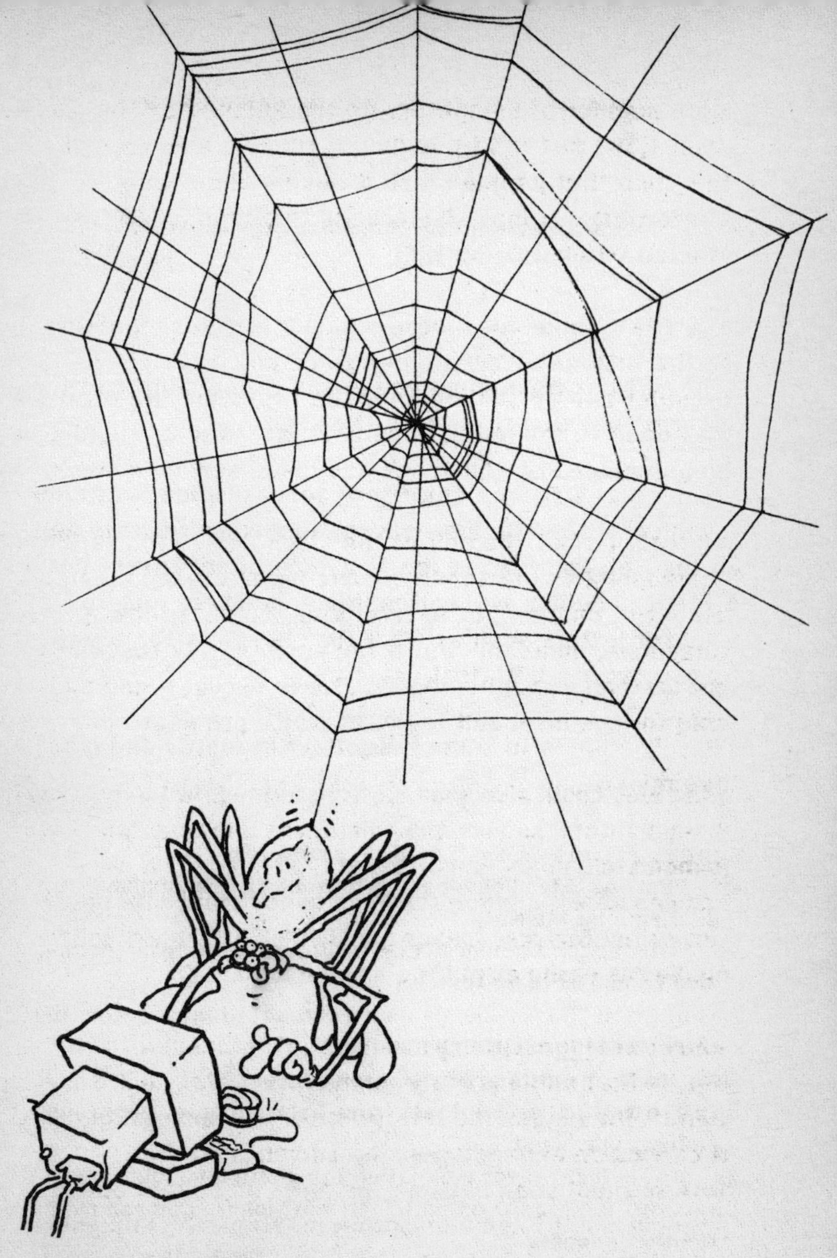

> Over and out!

Netspeak

> The Net has its own language and if you want to surf in style, you've got to learn the lingo.

> As well as TLAs and emoticons there are loads of new technical words. Be warned: spelling is notoriously bad on the Net. Sometimes this is due to typing errors but often it is deliberate. For example, numbers may be used for letters such as «3» for «e»; or «8» for «ate», as in L8R (later).

> Here's a guide to some essential Net words and what they mean:

Access provider See **Service provider**.

Anonymous FTP Downloading files which are available to everyone on the Net.

ASCII American Standard Code for Information Interchange, also known as plain text.

Bandwidth This is the maximum amount of information that can be sent through a connection.

Bot Programs with artificial intelligence.

Bounced Mail e-mail that comes back because the wrong address was used.

Browser A client for navigating the World Wide Web.

Channel A «room» on an IRC channel where you can chat to other people.

Client A program which allows you to use a server. For example, the software which you use to pick up e-mail is called an e-mail client.

TLA //TLA@page61
emoticons //Emoticons@page21

Cross post To send the same posting to more than one newsgroup.

Cyberspace The virtual world of the Internet.

Domain name A name of an address on the Internet.

e-mail The system that allows you to send messages to other people on the Net.

e-zine Like a magazine - only on the Internet!

FAQ Frequently Asked Questions - a list of the most common questions and their answers, found in newsgroups and on some Web pages.

File Transfer Protocol (FTP) The main way of downloading files across the Net.

Finger A program that gives you information about someone else who is on-line.

Flame A crushing put-down or nasty remark.

Flamebait Someone who deserves to be flamed!

Gopher A vast collection of Internet archives similar to the Web.

Host The computer to which you connect, in order to access the Net.

HTML Hyper Text Mark-up Language, used to write/program Web pages.

IP number A series of numbers that (like a Domain name) locates a computer on the Net.

Keypals Just like penpals - only you write to them using e-mail!

Kill file A way of blocking out some newsgroups or articles posted by someone you don't like.

Login Connecting to your service provider and going on-line.

Logoff Disconnecting from your service provider and returning to RL.

Lurkers Net users who read other people's messages in newgroups but do not post any of their own.

Mirror site A site on the Net which has exactly the same contents as another site to help spread or share the load.

Moderated A channel or newsgroup which is supervised.

MUD Multi-User Dimension, a virtual world, rather like IRC channels but much more detailed, in which you can play games.

Newbie Someone who is new to the Net.

Newsgroup A discussion group on Usenet.

Newsreader A client that allows you to access newsgroups.

Nick Your nickname on the Internet.

Poster Someone who leaves messages in a newsgroup.

Protocol The language used by computers to «talk» to each other.

Server A computer that allows you to connect to it using a client. Your service provider has lots of servers.

Service provider Also known as an Access provider, a company that sells access to the Internet.

Signature Your personal way of signing off at the end of postings and e-mail.

Snail mail Letters delivered by the postman.

Spam To send someone junk e-mail, or leave useless postings in a newsgroup.

Telnet A protocol which allows you to log on to another computer on the Net and run programs on that computer.

Thread A group of messages with the same topic in a newsgroup.

Timeout When your computer automatically disconnects because you are not using the connection.

URL Uniform Resource Locator, the address of a page on the World Wide Web, FTP sites or e-mail.

Usenet A vast network of newsgroups.

World Wide Web A network of files with both text and graphics on the Net that can be accessed using a browser.